▪SCHOLASTIC
READ & RESPOND

Bringing the best books to life in the classroom

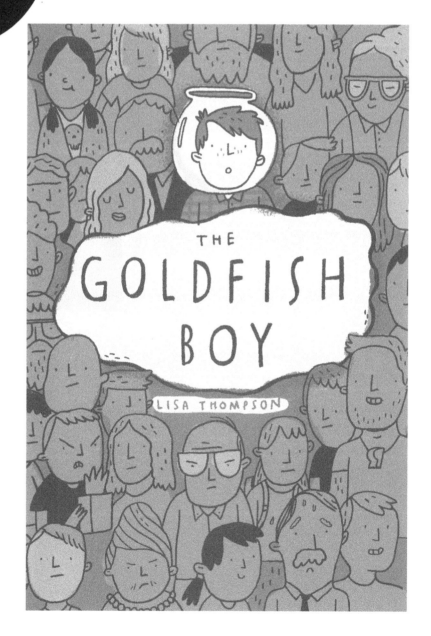

THE GOLDFISH BOY

LISA THOMPSON

FOR AGES 7–11

Published in the UK by Scholastic, 2021
Book End, Range Road, Witney, Oxfordshire, OX29 0YD
Scholastic Ireland, 89E Lagan Road, Dublin Industrial Estate, Glasnevin, Dublin, D11 HP5F

SCHOLASTIC and associated logos are trademarks and/or registered trademarks of Scholastic Inc.

www.scholastic.co.uk

© 2021 Scholastic Limited

1 2 3 4 5 6 7 8 9   1 2 3 4 5 6 7 8 9 0

A CIP catalogue record for this book is available from the British Library.
ISBN 978-1407-18393-0

Printed and bound by Ashford Colour Press
Paper made from wood grown in sustainable forests and other controlled sources.

Extracts from *The National Curriculum in England, English Programme of Study* © Crown Copyright. Reproduced under the terms of the Open Government Licence (OGL). http://www.nationalarchives.gov.uk/doc/open-government-licence/version/3

Authors Jillian Powell
Editorial team Vicki Yates, Suzanne Adams, Julia Roberts
Series designer Dipa Mistry
Typesetter QBS Learning
Illustrator Belinda Chen Astound US Inc

Acknowledgements
The publishers gratefully acknowledge permission to reproduce the following material:
Scholastic Children's Books for the use of the text extracts and cover from *The Goldfish Boy* written by Lisa Thompson

Every effort has been made to trace copyright holders for the works reproduced in this book, and the publishers apologise for any inadvertent omissions.

CONTENTS

How to use Read & Respond in your classroom...

Read & Respond provides teaching ideas related to a specific well-loved children's book. Each Read & Respond book is divided into the following sections:

ABOUT THE BOOK AND AUTHOR

Gives you some background information about the book and the author.

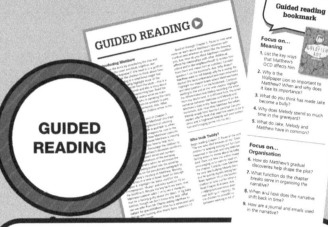

GUIDED READING

Breaks the book down into sections and gives notes for using it with guided reading groups. A bookmark has been provided on page 12 containing comprehension questions. The children can be directed to refer to these as they read.

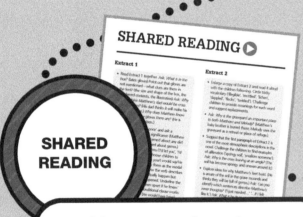

SHARED READING

Provides extracts from the children's book with associated notes for focused work. There is also one non-fiction extract that relates to the children's book.

GRAMMAR, PUNCTUATION & SPELLING

Provides word-level work related to the children's book so you can teach grammar, punctuation and spelling in context.

PLOT, CHARACTER & SETTING

Contains activity ideas focused on the plot, characters and the setting of the story.

PLOT, CHARACTER AND SETTING ▶

TALK ABOUT IT

Has speaking and listening activities related to the children's book. These activities may be based directly on the children's book or be broadly based on the themes and concepts of the story.

GET WRITING

Provides writing activities related to the children's book. These activities may be based directly on the children's book or be broadly based on the themes and concepts of the story.

ASSESSMENT

Contains short activities that will help you assess whether the children have understood concepts and curriculum objectives. They are designed to be informal activities to feed into your planning.

Activities

The activities follow the same format:

- **Objective:** the objective for the lesson. It will be based upon a curriculum objective, but will often be more specific to the focus being covered.

- **What you need:** a list of resources you need to teach the lesson, including photocopiable pages.

- **What to do:** the activity notes.

- **Differentiation:** this is provided where specific and useful differentiation advice can be given to support and/or extend the learning in the activity. Differentiation by providing additional adult support has not been included as this will be at a teacher's discretion based upon specific children's needs and ability, as well as the availability of support.

The activities are numbered for reference within each section and should move through the text sequentially – so you can use the lesson while you are reading the book. Once you have read the book, most of the activities can be used in any order you wish.

❝The titles are great fun to use and cover exactly the range of books that children most want to read. It makes it easy to explore texts fully and ensure the children want to keep on reading more.❞

Chris Flanagan, Year 5 Teacher, St Thomas of Canterbury Primary School

CURRICULUM LINKS

Section	Activity	Curriculum objectives
Guided reading		Comprehension: To ask questions to improve their understanding.
Shared reading	1	Comprehension: To check that the book makes sense to them, discussing their understanding and exploring the meaning of words in context; to provide reasoned justifications for their views.
	2	Comprehension: To discuss and evaluate how authors use language, including figurative language, considering the impact on the reader.
	3	Comprehension: To discuss and evaluate how authors use language, including figurative language, considering the impact on the reader.
	4	Comprehension: To identify how language, structure and presentation contribute to meaning.
Grammar, punctuation & spelling	1	Grammar: To use modal verbs or adverbs to indicate degrees of possibility.
	2	Grammar: To use expanded noun phrases to convey complicated information concisely.
	3	Grammar: To use passive verbs to affect the presentation of information in a sentence.
	4	Transcription: To distinguish between homophones and other words which are often confused.
	5	Grammar: To use relative clauses beginning with who, which, where, when, whose, that or with an implied relative pronoun.
	6	Punctuation: To use colons to introduce a list; to punctuate bullet points consistently.
Plot, character & setting	1	Comprehension: To identify and discuss themes and conventions in and across a wide range of writing.
	2	Composition: To consider how authors have developed…settings in what pupils have read.
	3	Comprehension: To identify how…structure…contribute to meaning; to make comparisons within books.
	4	Comprehension: To predict what might happen from details stated and implied.
	5	Comprehension: To draw inferences such as inferring characters' feelings, thoughts and motives from their actions, and justifying inferences with evidence.
	6	Composition: To consider how authors have developed…settings in what pupils have read.
	7	Spoken language: To participate…in role play… Composition: To consider how authors have developed characters in what pupils have read.
	8	Composition: To consider how authors have developed…settings in what pupils have read. Comprehension: To identify and discuss themes and conventions in and across a wide range of writing.

Section	Activity	Curriculum objectives
Talk about it	1	Spoken language: To give well-structured descriptions, explanations and narratives for different purposes, including for expressing feelings.
	2	Spoken language: To develop understanding through speculating, hypothesising, imagining and exploring ideas.
	3	Spoken language: To articulate and justify answers, arguments and opinions.
	4	Comprehension: To distinguish between statements of fact and opinion. Spoken language: To articulate and justify answers, arguments and opinions.
	5	Spoken language: To ask relevant questions to extend their understanding and knowledge.
	6	Spoken language: To maintain attention and participate actively in collaborative conversations, staying on topic and initiating and responding to comments. Comprehension: To discuss and evaluate how authors use language, including figurative language, considering the impact on the reader.
Get writing	1	Composition: To consider how authors have developed…settings in what pupils have read; to describe settings…
	2	Comprehension: To discuss and evaluate how authors use language, including figurative language, considering the impact on the reader. Composition: To select appropriate vocabulary, understanding how such choices can change and enhance meaning.
	3	Composition: To identify the audience for and purpose of the writing, selecting the appropriate form and using other similar writing as models for their own.
	4	Composition: To draft and write by précising longer passages.
	5	Composition: To identify the audience for and purpose of the writing, selecting the appropriate form and using other similar writing as models for their own.
	6	Composition: To use…organisational and presentational devices to structure text and to guide the reader (for example, headings, bullet points, underlining).
Assessment	1	Comprehension: To ask questions to improve their understanding.
	2	Grammar: To use modal verbs or adverbs to indicate degrees of possibility.
	3	Comprehension: To identify and discuss themes and conventions in and across a wide range of writing.
	4	Spoken language: To articulate and justify answers, arguments and opinions.
	5	Composition: To draft and write by précising longer passages.
	6	Composition: To use…organisational and presentational devices to structure text and to guide the reader (for example, headings, bullet points, underlining).

Key facts

The Goldfish Boy

⊙ **Author**
Lisa Thompson

⊙ **First published:**
2017 by Scholastic

⊙ **Did you know?**
The title character in the book suffers a mental disorder which affects around 12 in 1000 people.

About the book

The Goldfish Boy is Lisa Thompson's debut novel. It has won wide acclaim, becoming a best seller and gaining nominations for prizes including the Carnegie Medal and Waterstones Children's Book Prize. The central character, 12-year-old Matthew Corbin, is confined to his bedroom with crippling OCD (obsessive-compulsive disorder). His fear of dirt and germs leaves him isolated from family and friends, and he spends his time watching the neighbours on Chestnut Close, logging their movements in his diary. His meticulous attention to their daily routines leads him to discover the sinister disappearance of a toddler from the house next door. Matthew must struggle to overcome his personal demons to solve the mystery of the child's abduction. The storyline echoes the famous Alfred Hitchcock thriller movie *Rear Window*, released in 1954, in which a photographer is confined to his New York apartment with a broken leg. Watching his neighbours in the surrounding blocks to alleviate his boredom, he witnesses the disappearance of a woman and turns detective to discover her murderer, putting his own life in danger. *The Goldfish Boy* combines elements of a thriller and detective novel with a sensitive portrayal of a boy struggling to manage a mental health problem. As the plot unravels, clues, suspects, red herrings and evidence must be weighed up and assessed by Matthew and the reader. Through the first-person narrative, we begin to understand why Matthew feels and acts as he does and the strategies that finally help him overcome his demons.

About the author

Lisa Thompson was born in Essex. She worked as a broadcast assistant for BBC Radio 2 and then for an independent production company, before becoming a full-time writer. As a child, she remembers wanting to become a singer (recording herself on her cassette player) or to work in film production. But she always enjoyed writing and completed her first story – about a girl who started a rescue centre for horses – when she was nine years old. She lives with her family and an adopted black cat in Suffolk, and she writes sitting at the dining-room table where she can see the garden and is within reach of the kettle and biscuits! She has described the routine of her writing day as framed between the morning and afternoon school runs, going shopping and ferrying the children to football matches, all the while trying to resist temptations of going online or doing other tasks in order to focus on her writing. Her novels typically focus on a child struggling to overcome mental health or other issues, in settings which combine mystery and imagination with the everyday. Her debut novel was followed by *The Light Jar*, a novel which tackles the subject of domestic abuse and re-visits the theme of a sensitive boy facing his fears. Her novels are now translated into many languages and sold all over the world. She also travels around the country doing school visits and writing workshops to inspire others to enjoy creative writing.

GUIDED READING ▶

Introducing Matthew

Introduce the book by considering the title and examining the cover and blurb together. Ask: *What sets the boy apart?* (His head is in a goldfish bowl.) Encourage the children to think about how a goldfish swimming in a small bowl might feel (trapped, bored). Briefly highlight some of the clues to the novel's genre from the blurb – this is a mystery story, a whodunnit and also a story about finding friendship and overcoming fear. Read the first chapter together and review what we learn about the boy, Matthew, who is narrating the story (he watches neighbours from his window to pass the time and logs their movements). Ask: *What unusual event happens?* (Two children arrive in the house next door.)

Continue reading to the end of Chapter 2. Ask: *What do we learn about Matthew?* (He stays in his room because he is frightened of catching germs.) *Who does he confide in and talk to when he is alone?* (a lion that he imagines he sees in the torn wallpaper) Talk about how Matthew's parents feel. (They are worried because Matthew is missing school and they don't know how to help him.) Read Chapter 3 at pace. Encourage the children to identify evidence of Matthew's obsessive condition, such as his focus on exact detail and number. Reflect how his observations of the everyday become more dramatic when he witnesses the toddler, Teddy, being pushed into the pond by his sister. Pause on the penultimate paragraph to highlight Casey's mockery of Matthew, likening him to a fish in a tank or bowl. Read on through Chapter 4. Highlight the italics used for the onomatopoeic *'thump'* and raise question 10 on the bookmark. Review the key facts we learn: that Matthew's parents want him to see a therapist; that he is feeling guilty about the death of his baby brother, though we don't know why. Ask: *What can we infer from Mr Charles asking Matthew to babysit his grandchildren?* (that he is exhausted and fed up with looking after them) Raise question 13 on the bookmark.

Read on through Chapter 5. Pause to note what more we learn about Matthew's obsession with numbers and attention to detail (like the drawing pin). Ask: *How do you think Matthew's condition affects his relationships with other children at school and in the neighbourhood?* (It isolates him from them and makes him an outsider.) Consider question 1 on the bookmark. Ask: *Why doesn't Matthew want to tell Melody why he is seeing the doctor?* (He feels embarrassed and even ashamed.) Highlight the chapter break where Matthew faints and raise question 7 on the bookmark. Continue reading to the end of the next chapter. Highlight the differentiated text (italics) recording the letter from the doctor and, in a different font, the email exchange between Matthew and Melody and Matthew's diary entry. Raise question 9 on the bookmark. Ask: *How does Matthew feel when Melody emails him?* (worried, panicky) *Can you explain why he feels that way?* (He wants to be left alone and is frightened Melody will start bothering him and bringing germs into his life.)

Who took Teddy?

Begin reading Chapter 7. Pause at the sentence 'The one who died because of me.' Encourage the children to keeping looking out for clues about what happened in the past and why Matthew gets a bad feeling when he thinks about his baby brother who died. Point out how the author keeps us guessing – encouraging us to want to read on. Finish reading the chapter. Consider how Matthew feels torn when he sees Jake bullying Melody (he wants to help her, but he quickly regrets letting her into the house). Raise question 14 on the bookmark, encouraging the children to look out for other examples as they read. Read Chapter 8 at pace. Ask: *How does the storyline suddenly become more dramatic?* (The toddler next door goes missing.) Read on, encouraging the children to consider how Matthew is again torn between wanting to be of help and battling his own problems. Ask: *How do you think Matthew feels when PC Campen overhears the phone message in Chapter 9?* (He feels embarrassed.) Finish the chapter, reflecting on how the author creates 'suspects' in the neighbourhood. Invite the children to consider how the suspects function as another hook, making us want to read on – the plot has become a mystery or a whodunnit. Raise question 6 on the bookmark.

Begin reading Chapter 10, highlighting how the narrative shifts back into the past to describe Matthew's friendship with Jake. Highlight question 8 on the bookmark, telling children to look for other examples as they read. Ask: *Why does Matthew feel guilty?* (He did not stand up to Jake's bullies.) Ask question 3 on the bookmark. Note the 'cliffhanger' that makes us want to read on in the final sentence of the chapter. Encourage the children to speculate on who *they* think took Teddy Dawson, giving their reasons.

Clues, suspects and red herrings

Read on through Chapter 11. Ask: *Why do you think Mum needs a hug from Matthew?* (Someone else's son has gone missing.) *How do you think she feels when Matthew fails to respond?* (sad, bewildered)

Note how the narrative shifts back to the past again, then forward to the present, with the journalist's report in Chapter 12. As you read, notice how the italicised text is used to represent Matthew's thoughts. Discuss question 11 on the bookmark, encouraging the children to look out for other examples as they read. Ask: *Why is Melody hurt when she reads Matthew's journal?* (He lists her as a suspect.)

Read to the end of Chapter 12. Focus on the email exchange between Matthew and Melody and consider question 15 on the bookmark. Note the reference to Matthew's guilt over his baby brother. Pause at the beginning of the next chapter and ask a volunteer to explain the reference to 'Chapter 10 plus 3'. (Matthew is superstitious about the number 13 and thinks it is unlucky.)

Continue reading through the next two chapters. Ask: *Why is Matthew suspicious of Casey?* (He saw her push Teddy into the pond.) Suggest that when Matthew visits the therapist the whole family is feeling under stress. Ask: *What evidence is there for this?* (His parents argue; Matthew is on edge and struggling with the idea of number 13 and all the germs around him.) Highlight how he applies his same close observation to Dr Rhodes as he does to the neighbours. At the end of Chapter 14, ask a volunteer to explain Matthew's reference to 'one useless 12 year old'. (Matthew feels useless because he's been unable to find out who took Teddy.) Link the discussion to question 12 on the bookmark.

Read on, pausing to note the shift in time in the narrative. Ask: *Why does Matthew ask for Melody's help?* (He knows he can't ask his parents to get the latex gloves; he has no choice.) Read on to the end of the next chapter. Raise question 4 on the bookmark. Challenge a volunteer to explain the significance of the graveyard to Melody and to Matthew. (She uses it as a retreat; Matthew knows his baby brother is buried there.) Ask: *How does Matthew upset Melody this time?* (She confides in him, but he then accuses her of doing something wrong and disrespectful.) Reflect on how the author keeps us guessing about the prime suspects and also how Matthew's tentative friendship with Melody fluctuates.

Matthew's fears

Pause at the end of Chapter 17 to ask what we have learned about Matthew's fear of germs. (He is frightened of passing them on and harming others because he believes he caused Callum's death.) Note the shift in narrative to the past. As you read through the next few chapters, encourage the children to note how we are given 'leads' or 'clues' to prime suspects (such as Nina losing her own son) that are later revealed as 'red herrings' or false leads. At the end of Chapter 24, ask: *What is about to happen to Matthew's room?* (His father is re-decorating it and will destroy the Wallpaper Lion). Highlight Matthew's words in Chapter 27 '"You don't know what you've done!"' and ask a volunteer to explain them. (He has destroyed Matthew's confidante and companion.) Return to question 2 on the bookmark.

A crime solved

Continue reading. Pause at the end of Chapter 34 to ask: *What does Nina mean about dancing in the rain?* (You have to make the most of how things are, even if they are bad or difficult, and not just wait for them to change.) Raise question 16 on the bookmark. Ask: *What do we learn about Matthew's guilt towards Callum from his session with Dr Rhodes?* (He is convinced his mother lost the baby because he passed his germs on to her.) *Why does Matthew no longer need the Wallpaper Lion?* (He is at last able to share his fears with others.) Highlight how the family is able to relax and laugh together now that his parents know the truth. Reflect how Matthew feels now that he has been able to confide and share his fears.

Ask a volunteer to summarise how Matthew finally solves the crime and discovers the culprit. (He spots the toddler's handprint on the glass at Penny and Gordon's house.) Ask: *How does the change in the weather echo the relief that the residents feel?* (The heatwave breaks, bringing a thunderstorm.) Review the ending, focusing on how friendships have revived or been strengthened (Matthew, Melody and Jake). Consider question 5 on the bookmark. Ask: *How do you think Matthew feels at the end of the story? How has he changed since the beginning of the story?* (He is hopeful that he can change and begin to enjoy life again.) Discuss question 17 on the bookmark.

Guided reading bookmark

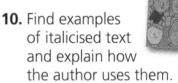

Focus on... Meaning

1. List the key ways that Matthew's OCD affects him.

2. Why is the Wallpaper Lion so important to Matthew? When and why does it lose its importance?

3. What do you think has made Jake become a bully?

4. Why does Melody spend so much time in the graveyard?

5. What do Jake, Melody and Matthew have in common?

Focus on... Organisation

6. How do Matthew's gradual discoveries help shape the plot?

7. What function do the chapter breaks serve in organising the narrative?

8. When and how does the narrative shift back in time?

9. How are a journal and emails used in the narrative?

Guided reading bookmark

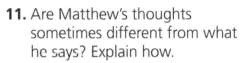

Focus on... Language and features

10. Find examples of italicised text and explain how the author uses them.

11. Are Matthew's thoughts sometimes different from what he says? Explain how.

12. Find examples of ways Matthew uses lists to organise his thoughts.

Focus on... Purpose, viewpoints and effects

13. Why do you think the author tells the story in the first person (Matthew's voice)?

14. Give examples of situations where Matthew is torn between his fears and his desire to help others.

15. What are the main sources of humour in the story?

16. Which characters in the story show the most understanding towards Matthew and which show the least?

17. What do we learn from Matthew's story? Who do you think would benefit most from reading it?

SHARED READING ▶

Extract 1

- Read Extract 1 together. Ask: *What is in the box?* (latex gloves) Point out that gloves are not mentioned – what clues are there in the text? (the size and shape of the box, the numbered contents, the illustration) Ask: *Why do you think Matthew's dad would be cross with his mum?* (His dad thinks it will make his condition worse.) *Why does Matthew know exactly how many gloves there are?* (He is obsessed with numbers.)

- Circle the phrase 'for once' and ask a volunteer to explain its significance (Matthew would normally be concerned about any dirt in his room and be worried about germs.) Circle the abbreviated forms ('I'd let you', 'I'd say', 'He'd have been'). Choose children to expand them. (I would let you/I would say/He would have been) Identify them as the modal verb 'would'. Consider how the verb describes something that didn't actually happen but might or could have happened. Underline the sentence: 'He'd have been upset if he knew.' Note how the 'if' or conditional clause works with the modal verb (He would have been). Ask: *Can you find another example of a modal verb in the extract?* ('I would have liked')

- Focus on the sentence beginning 'Not so much at me...' Point out that it has no main subject/verb. Ask: *Can you suggest why an incomplete sentence/informal style is appropriate here?* (Matthew is confiding in us, the reader, as if he is telling a friend his story.)

Extract 2

- Enlarge a copy of Extract 2 and read it aloud with the children following. Circle tricky vocabulary ('illegible', 'mottled', 'lichen', 'dappled', 'flecks', 'twisted'). Challenge children to provide meanings for each word and suggest replacements.

- Ask: *Why is the graveyard an important place to both Matthew and Melody?* (Matthew's baby brother is buried there; Melody uses the graveyard as a retreat or place of refuge.)

- Suggest that the first paragraph of Extract 2 is one of the most atmospheric descriptions in the novel. Challenge the children to find examples of alliteration ('spongy soil', 'swallow someone'). Ask: *Why is the cross leaning at an angle?* (The soil has become spongy and uneven around it.)

- Explore ideas for why Matthew's feet twist. (He is aware of the soil in the grave mounds and thinks they will be full of germs.) Ask: *Can you identify which sentences describe Matthew's inner thoughts?* ('I just needed...' '...if I felt like it.') Ask: *What is he trying to do here?* (reassure himself that he can soon get away and get clean again) Invite children to describe how Matthew and Melody are each feeling. (Matthew is uncomfortable and tense; Melody is hopeful and excited because she wants to show him her treasured find.) Ask: *Which words convey these feelings?* Circle 'edged', 'twisted', 'beaming' and explore their meanings. Discuss what they tell us about each character.

- Can they recall what Melody wants to show Matthew? (the mermaid on the grave) Ask: *What do you think it shows?* (Melody feels she can confide in Matthew; she wants to be his friend and wants to share something special with him.)

Extract 3

- Read Extract 3 together. Ask a volunteer to explain Matthew's shocking discovery: his father is stripping the wallpaper in his bedroom. Ask: *Why might Matthew's parents expect him to be pleased?* (They think he would like a clean, freshly-decorated room.) *Why is Matthew upset and shocked?* (His father is about to destroy the Wallpaper Lion.)

- Underline the sentence 'He'd always been there for me, day and night.' Invite the children to explain what Matthew means. (The Wallpaper Lion is Matthew's secret companion; he talks to him; he confides in him.) Ask them to identify language that personifies the lion ('cowering in his little corner', 'tears streamed out of his drooping eye').

- Circle the words on the extract that are in italics and capitals. Ask: *What is their function?* (emphasis; Matthew is shouting) Challenge the children to identify an onomatopoeic word (*'shlump'*). Ask: *What does it convey?* (the sound of wet wallpaper slumping onto the ground) Focus on the descriptive language in the extract. Challenge the children to pick out two similes ('bubbled away again like a boiling kettle'; 'peeled away like curls of soft butter'). Encourage them to notice how the author uses sights and sounds to convey the scene. Ask: *Which words suggest sounds?* ('bubbling', 'scraped') Highlight how a single word is used as a sentence (*'SCRAPE'*) Ask: *What effect does this have?* (It emphasises the sound.)

- Underline the phrase 'one clean sweep'. Ask: *What does it mean here?* (in a single, complete piece) Challenge the children to suggest how the phrase is used in a figurative way (meaning an overwhelming success, for example, Matthew made a clean sweep of the family rounders games).

Extract 4

- Together, read Extract 4. Ask a volunteer to summarise the two opposing perspectives on germs (as dangerous monsters that invade our homes but also as friendly organisms vital to our health). Ask: *Which is Matthew's view?* (They are monsters, to be feared and killed.)

- Encourage the children to cite and describe any advertisements they have seen showing germs as little monsters. Do they think that the adverts are effective? How do they make us feel? Ask: *Have you heard of 'friendly' bacteria and ways we can support them and help our health?* Again, encourage the children to cite advertisements they may have seen for probiotic yoghurts and drinks.

- Circle tricky vocabulary, challenging children to provide meanings and suggest alternatives ('miniscule', 'tentacles', 'contaminate', 'organisms', 'nurture'). Focus on the adjectives: 'humanoid', 'reptilian' and 'insectoid'. Choose volunteers to extract their meaning (like humans, reptiles, insects) and note the suffixes (-oid,- ian). Tell them that the suffixes here mean 'resembling'.

- Challenge the children to pick out words from the extract that suggest germs are a dangerous enemy ('hoard', 'monsters', 'menacing', 'lurk', 'contaminate'). Ask: *Which words suggest the opposite?* ('vital', 'helping', 'protect', 'friendly', 'sensitive'). Focus on the metaphor of fighting a war, Ask: *What are our 'weapons'?* Pick out figurative language describing them. Ask: *What are cleaning sprays likened to?* (guns) *Can you pick out examples of alliteration?* ('miniscule monsters'; 'swarm and scurry', 'spray and scour') Challenge the children to expand each phrase with another alliterative adjective (miniscule, menacing monsters; swarm, scatter and scurry; spray, scrub and scour).

Extract 1

Under my bed I had a secret box.

I would have liked to say it was a mysterious old wooden box that I'd found buried in the garden, smuggled upstairs and hidden behind the folds of my duvet. It would sit there patiently, keeping its treasures locked inside. Once I knew I could trust you, I'd let you kneel beside me as I carefully opened the crumbling lid. Clumps of mud would fall on to my carpet but, for once, I wouldn't care. Your mouth would drop open, your eyes getting wider and wider as you gazed at the riches inside.

I wished my secret box was like that.

But it wasn't.

My box was clinical. It was made of white-and-grey cardboard and was the size and shape of a small shoebox with an oval hole in the top. The manufacturer's name was printed around the sides and in the bottom corner at each end it read, in bold black type:

Contents: 100

I'd say there were probably around thirty left.

When I say *probably* I mean *exactly*. There were exactly thirty left.

Mum knew all about my secret box but Dad didn't. He'd have been upset if he knew. Not so much at me, but more at Mum for "encouraging" me.

"It's not right, Sheila. What're you doing giving him stuff like that for, eh? You're just making him worse."

That was how Dad would react.

He wouldn't understand that life for me at the moment, without that box, was impossible.

Extract 2

This part of the graveyard was overgrown and the ground was uneven where the coffins had rotted away, leaving spongy soil ready to swallow someone up. Most of the stones were illegible, their surfaces mottled with lime-green lichen. I spotted Melody behind a cross that was leaning at an awkward angle.

"Oh good, you're here!" she said and she glanced at my hands but didn't say anything.

"I've just come to say thanks again for getting the gloves but I'm going back now. I'm not feeling great and I think I've tried to do too much. I feel dizzy. I need some water, I think."

As Melody stood with her hands on her hips the dappled sunlight danced around her, picking out the flecks of auburn in her hair.

"But you've come this far! Honestly, it's really worth it. Just come over, have a quick look, and then go. OK?"

She crouched next to a grave and pulled at some weeds. I just needed to walk five more paces, see what it was, then run home, sprint home. I could go straight upstairs and into the shower. It'd be fine. I could clean my room, wait for the hot water to warm up again, then have another shower if I felt like it. I edged my way towards her and she turned to me, her face beaming. My feet twisted as the mounds of earth pressed against the thin soles of my shoes. I stood at the other side of the grave from her, my gloved hands tucked under my arms.

"Look," she whispered. "Have you ever seen anything so beautiful?"

Extract 3

He lifted the steamer off and with his other hand, scraped the paper away in one clean sweep. The yellowing strands fell to the floor in a wet *shlump*. He moved the steamer down the wall, and it bubbled away again like a boiling kettle.

"Stop it! Stop it, Dad," I said, but I said it too quietly.

"Mum's going to make up a bed in the office for you for a couple of nights," he said loudly over the noises and the radio. "You won't want to sleep in here with all this mess, eh?"

Behind him I could see the Wallpaper Lion, cowering in his little corner. A line of sweat was seeping through Dad's T-shirt making a dark trail down his spine.

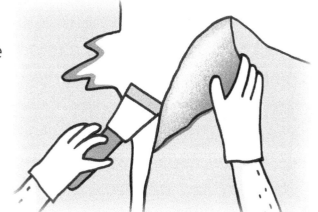

"B-but I didn't want you to decorate. Why are you doing this? IT'S MY ROOM!"

I wondered if I could just push him off the steps and put a stop to the whole thing. He scraped another section and the paper peeled away like curls of soft butter.

"Don't be silly, Matthew," he said without looking at me. "It needs doing. And it'll be nice and clean then, just how you like it!"

SCRAPE.

Another strand fell to the floor. Behind him the steamer was just centimetres away from the Wallpaper Lion's mane. Condensation glistened across the paper and tears streamed out of his drooping eye and down his flat, wide nose. He'd always been there for me, day and night. What would I do without him? I ran to the ladder just as Dad placed the square, plastic steamer over the lion's face.

"No! Please! Take it off! TAKE IT OFF!"

Extract 4

by Jillian Powell

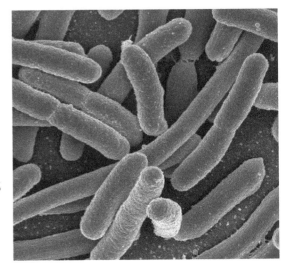

A hoard of miniscule monsters is invading our homes. Many are humanoid in shape, some reptilian or insectoid; others just menacing blobs of purple and green, resembling aliens from outer space. They have limbs and sometimes tentacles; huge, angry eyes and jaws full of jagged teeth. They lurk under plugs and beneath toilet seats, cluster on doorknobs and even contaminate our kitchen worktops and phone screens. How do we protect ourselves against them? We produce weapons, clinical bottles and sprays of gels, soaps, fluids, foams and powders. We take aim, pull the trigger and shoot. The tiny invaders swarm and scurry, their angry eyes flashing, their teeth gnashing. We have declared war on the enemy, armed with powerful – *kills 99.9% of viruses and bacteria* – anti-bacterial sprays and sanitisers.

We spend £50 billion a year on cleaning products to fight the bacteria and viruses that live in our homes. We know that these tiny, living organisms can get inside our bodies and cause illness and disease. But viewed under a microscope, how true is our fictional image of them? In reality, their shapes are often neatly symmetrical and geometric, based on rods, spheres, helixes and polyhedrons. And not all bacteria are monsters intent on harming us. Some are vital to our health. Trillions of friendly bacteria live in our digestive systems, helping us absorb nutrients, fight infections and protect us against bad bacteria. Our bodies need these friendly bacteria to help protect and repair our cells and fight off illnesses and diseases.

So while we clean and wipe, spray and scour, we must also remember to nurture our friendly bacteria, eating healthy foods like fruits and vegetables and yoghurts. Scientists have found that friendly bacteria that live in our gut are very sensitive and can even be affected by noise and stress. So, look after them; bacteria are not all monsters.

GRAMMAR, PUNCTUATION & SPELLING ▶

1. What if?

Objective
To use modal verbs or adverbs to indicate degrees of possibility.

What you need
Copies of *The Goldfish Boy*, copies of Extract 1, photocopiable page 22 'What if?'

What to do
- Re-read Extract 1 together. Challenge the children to identify all the uses of the modal verb 'would' and underline or circle them: 'would have liked', 'would sit', 'would fall', 'wouldn't care', 'would drop', 'would react', 'wouldn't understand'. Ensure that they include the abbreviated form and know how to expand it, for example, He'd have = He would have.

- Discuss together what these verbs describe (something that didn't actually happen but which *could* or *might* have happened). Matthew is speculating or imagining things that were possible, even probable, though they didn't happen. He imagines how people would react if his box of gloves were an old treasure chest and he predicts how his dad would react if he discovered the gloves. Explain that we use a range of modal verbs: can/could, may/might, must, will/would and shall/should to indicate things that are or were possible.

- Arrange the children into pairs and hand out photocopiable page 22 'What if?' Give the children time to complete the sentences. Then bring the class back together and invite volunteers to read aloud their sentences. Challenge pairs to suggest adverbs to support and add emphasis to the modal verbs.

Differentiation
Support: Read together another passage, such as Matthew's speculation on Callum from Chapter 7, to practise identifying modal verbs.

Extension: Let pairs draft more sentences about characters in the novel using modal verbs.

2. Neat descriptions

Objective
To use expanded noun phrases to convey complicated information concisely.

What you need
Copies of *The Goldfish Boy*; photocopiable page 23 'Neat descriptions'.

What to do
- Read together the description of the Wallpaper Lion in Chapter 2. Challenge the children to pick out all the adjectives and adjectival phrases that describe what the lion is and isn't like, including his features, and write them on the board: (not) 'fierce', (not) a 'king of the jungle', 'funny-looking', 'gummy', 'scruffy', 'long', 'flat', 'drooping'.

- Point out how the author uses adjectives to compose longer phrases to describe the lion's mane, nose and eyes. Explain that we call these phrases 'expanded noun phrases'. Challenge the children to reword the description without using the expanded noun phrases (The lion didn't look fierce; he didn't look like a king of the jungle; he looked funny and gummy.) Reflect how the expanded noun phrases are a much neater and more concise way of helping us to visualise the Wallpaper Lion.

- Arrange the children into pairs and hand out photocopiable page 23 'Neat descriptions'. Allow them time to complete the page then bring the class back together to review their work, encouraging feedback to decide the most effective expanded noun phrases.

Differentiation
Support: Scan a chapter as a class to identify expanded noun phrases.

Extension: Tell pairs to repeat the exercise using one or more additional chapters.

3. Passives in action

Objective
To use passive verbs to affect the presentation of information in a sentence.

What you need
Copies of *The Goldfish Boy*.

What to do

- Write on the board two sentences: 'Casey pushed Teddy into the pond.' and 'Teddy was pushed by Casey into the pond.' Underline the active and passive verbs. Ask: *What difference does the verb form make?* (The active puts the emphasis on Casey, the passive puts the emphasis on Teddy.) Reflect that 'active' suggests action and intent; 'passive' suggests inaction or even helplessness. Ask: *Which sentence best conveys Casey is a bully?* (The active: she deliberately pushes him.) *Which best conveys Teddy's helplessness as a toddler?* (the passive) Suggest that, in this way, the verb form can sometimes affect the reader's inference.

- Write on the board: 'Fear trapped Matthew.' Choose a child to change the verb to a passive. (Matthew was trapped by fear.) Discuss the difference in inference conveyed: the active verb explains *what* is affecting him; the passive puts more emphasis on *how* Matthew is affected: Ask: *Which verb form best reflects Matthew's helplessness?* (the passive)

- Arrange the children into pairs. Tell them to compose short sentences about characters from the novel using active verbs. They should challenge their writing partner to convert the verb into the passive, then decide which form works best and why.

- Bring the class back together and ask volunteers to read aloud their sentences. Write some of the best suggestions on the board.

Differentiation
Support: Provide a list of sentences about characters using active verbs for children to convert to passive.

Extension: Challenge children to scan one chapter, identifying active and passive verbs and exploring their inference.

4. Confused or not?

Objective
To distinguish between homophones and other words that are often confused.

What you need
Copies of *The Goldfish Boy*.

What to do

- Write the word 'board' on the board in capital letters. Ask the children if they can think of its homophone – another word that sounds the same but has a different spelling and meaning (bored). Allow the children time to work in pairs to draft two short sentences about someone or something in the novel, using each word and its homophone to bring out the meaning, for example, Matthew felt bored alone in his room; Matthew did not want to touch the board.

- Write on the board 'Matthew said "Hi" to Melody.' Ask: *Can you find a homophone for one of the words in the sentence?* (high) Challenge the children to use it in a sentence about the novel, for example, The Wallpaper Lion was high up on the bedroom wall.

- Brainstorm with the class some more examples of homophones and write them on the board (wood/would, week/weak, aloud/allowed, know/no, where/wear and so on). Invite pairs of children to repeat the exercise, using the listed homophones in short sentences about the novel to bring out their meaning. For example, Matthew didn't know where Melody was going; Melody would often wear her black cardigan.

- Bring the class back together to share their sentences, asking volunteers to suggest the homophone before the second sentence is presented.

Differentiation
Support: Provide pairs of short sentences. Challenge children to identify the homophones then draft their own short sentences about the novel.

Extension: Challenge children to find more homophones of their own and use them to draft more sentences about the novel.

5. My relatives

Objective
To use relative clauses.

What you need
Copies of *The Goldfish Boy*, photocopiable page 24 'My relatives'.

What to do
- Focus on the character of Melody. Arrange the children into pairs and ask them to draft two short, factual statements about Melody. For example: Melody lived on the same street as Matthew; Melody went to the same school as Matthew; Melody wanted to be friends with Matthew; Melody liked to visit the graveyard. Bring the class together and write some of their suggestions on the board. Challenge the children to think how to join two of the sentences together to avoid the repetition of Melody as the subject. For example, Melody, who lived on the same street as Matthew, liked to visit the graveyard.

- Repeat the activity using a subject such as Matthew's secret box. For example, write on the board 'Matthew had a secret box.' Challenge the children to extend the statement using a relative pronoun – Matthew had a secret box which he kept under his bed. Underline the relative clauses and point out how they can tell us more about the subject in a concise way.

- Hand out photocopiable page 24 'My relatives' and let the children work individually or in pairs to complete the activity.

Differentiation
Support: Brainstorm some facts about each subject on the photocopiable page to help children create their clauses.

Extension: Challenge children to compose pairs of sentences about characters or topics in the novel then join them using relative clauses.

6. List the evidence

Objectives
To use colons to introduce a list; to punctuate bullet points consistently.

What you need
Copies of *The Goldfish Boy*.

What to do
- Challenge the children to name all the characters who become suspects for kidnapping Teddy. List the names on the board using a heading ('Suspects') a colon and bullet points. Invite the children to suggest alternative ways of listing (using a hyphen instead of or with the colon; using letters or numbers instead of bullets).

- Arrange the children into small groups. Allocate each group one of the suspects (Mr Charles, Penny, Mr Jenkins, Matthew, Melody and so on). Challenge them to skim and scan the novel, finding any facts or character traits that make them suspects. They should set out the facts as a list, using a colon and bullet points.

- When they have finished, bring the class back together and, using each character name as a heading, consolidate their findings on the board, listing key reasons why each is suspected. Consider how lists help present information in a neat, concise way. Ask a volunteer from each group to explain how Matthew's lists feature in the novel (summarising facts he has found out). Encourage the children to discuss why lists might be especially important to Matthew given his OCD. (Lists help him to organise his thoughts and to feel in control.)

Differentiation
Support: Provide groups with chapter or page references for their character.

Extension: Challenge children to devise and compile more lists using content from the novel, for example, the residents on Chestnut Close.

What if?

- Use your knowledge of the novel to complete these sentences using a modal verb.

If Nigel climbed onto his lap, Matthew _____

_____.

If Matthew accused Melody of taking Teddy, she _____

_____.

If his parents knew why Matthew feared germs so much, they _____

_____.

- Think of an 'if' clause to complete these sentences.

Matthew would be thrilled if _____.

Matthew's mum would be cross if _____.

Melody would be upset if _____.

- Choose one sentence from each group and add a supporting adverb.

1. _____

_____.

2. _____

_____.

Neat descriptions

- Draw a line to match each expanded noun phrase to the object it describes in the novel.
- Use the space underneath the pictures to write another expanded noun phrase describing each object.

three beautifully carved

_____

_____

a mysterious

_____

_____

a small orange

_____

_____

the half-deflated

_____

_____

deliciously cold

_____

_____

My relatives

- Write a relative clause to complete each sentence. Use one of these relative pronouns:

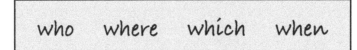

who   where   which   when

The doll, _____, had a porcelain face.

The graveyard, _____, was reached by an alley.

Jake, _____, had a skin condition called eczema.

Mr Charles, _____, enjoyed gardening.

The cake, _____, gave Mr Charles indigestion.

The time, _____, was sometime after 12.55 pm.

Teddy, _____, had gone missing.

Chestnut Close, _____, was on the news.

PLOT, CHARACTER AND SETTING ▶

1. What's his problem?

Objective
To identify and discuss themes and conventions in and across a wide range of writing.

What you need
Copies of *The Goldfish Boy*.

Cross-curricular link
PSHE

What to do

- Challenge the children to identify two main plot lines in the novel (Matthew's struggle to overcome OCD and the disappearance of Teddy Dawson). Invite them to identify and describe the two genres the novel combines (a realistic story with a mental health theme and a whodunnit or detective story). Encourage the children to think of other novels they have read which similarly combine different genres or themes, focusing on a mystery or crime to solve as well as the central character's own struggles (for example, *Artemis Fowl, Holes*).

- Ask: *How does each theme in* The Goldfish Boy *provide structure to the plot?* (Matthew has a problem to solve; we follow his efforts to solve or resolve the problem.) Organise the children into pairs and challenge them to work individually, each making notes on one problem Matthew has to solve. They should consider who helps him and how far he succeeds. Bring the class back together to share their findings.

- Focus on the ending of the novel. Discuss to what extent both problems are resolved and what is left for us to speculate about the future. (Teddy is found but Matthew is only just beginning his recovery from OCD.)

Differentiation
Support: Before pairs begin work, identify together the main characters who help Matthew.

2. Map it out

Objective
To consider how authors have developed settings in what pupils have read.

What you need
Copies of *The Goldfish Boy*, drawing materials.

Cross-curricular link
Geography

What to do

- Tell the children that they are going to try to draw a map of Chestnut Close. Before they begin, ask: *What kind of road is a 'close'?* (a road you enter and exit the same way, it is closed at one end)

- Arrange the class into pairs and tell them to scan the first chapter, making notes of facts: the number and type of houses, the names of residents, other places or features. Provide paper and drawing materials. Tell the children to use their notes to draw their map of Chestnut Close and label it with key features. Encourage them to include as much detail as possible, for example, linking the names of residents to the house numbers. They can scan other chapters to add information about the wider area, for example, the location of the graveyard or the direction of the High Street.

- Invite pairs to present their maps and then compare and contrast them. The children should consider which maps are the most accurate, easily understood or best presented and why. Ask: *Do the maps enhance our appreciation of the novel and if so, how?* Encourage feedback. Allow groups time to refine and improve their maps and display the most successful ones.

Differentiation
Support: Scan for information as a class activity, making notes on the board before the children begin working on their maps.

Extension: Children could use computing skills to construct an alternative image of Chestnut Close, for example, a 3D image.

3. Before and after

Objectives
To identify how structure contributes to meaning; to make comparisons within books.

What you need
Copies of *The Goldfish Boy*.

What to do

- Explain to the children that they are going to investigate flashbacks in the novel, where the narrative returns to past events. Ask: *Can you give examples of past episodes which Matthew relates during the novel?* (when Jake is bullied on the bus, the family gathering and rounders match, the loss of baby Callum) Arrange the children into pairs and tell them to skim and scan the novel for further examples, noting page numbers and summarising the content, then bring the class back together and compile a list on the board.

- Together, read one or two of the passages from the novel, encouraging the children to note any evidence that signals a shift back in time – the verb tense moving to the past perfect ('Last year's picnic *had been* epic'); chapter breaks and/or a conjunctions – '*When* I was five we used to walk to school…')

- Let pairs choose one episode, ensuring all episodes are covered. Challenge the children to summarise the key information we learn. Bring the class back together to share their findings. Encourage discussion on what these passages contribute to the novel. Ask: *Do they help us understand characters better? Do they help us predict what might happen in the future?*

Differentiation
Support: Allocate a specific episode, giving pairs of children key words to look out for. Challenge them to summarise their episode with the help of the key words.

Extension: Challenge pairs of children to plot a timeline of events, including the flashbacks, in chronological order.

4. Plot hooks

Objective
To predict what might happen from details stated and implied.

What you need
Copies of *The Goldfish Boy*.

What to do

- Tell the children that they are going to focus on devices the author uses to keep the reader engaged and wanting to find out what happens next, for example, chapter breaks or questions raised at the end of a chapter. The statement that Teddy Dawson has gone missing (the last line of Chapter 8) tells us that the plot has taken a dramatic turn. Ask: *What can we now predict as readers?* (that the novel is evolving into a mystery/ detective story/ whodunnit)

- Arrange the children into small groups and assign them four or five chapters each. Tell them to examine chapter breaks and endings. Ask: *What can we predict will happen? What questions are left unanswered? Where does the author plant a 'red herring' or false lead? Where is there progress in the detective trail?* Write these questions on the board for the children to refer to during the activity. Each group should appoint a note taker to note down their ideas as they work.

- When they have scanned their chapters, encourage the groups to decide which chapter endings have the best 'hooks' to encourage us to read on.

- Bring the class back together. Invite children from each group to share their findings. Discuss how the author uses these hooks to keep us guessing and engaged.

Differentiation
Support: Assign key chapters, such as 10 and 33, for groups to focus on.

Extension: Encourage children to identify other 'hooks' within chapters, created by planting clues which can be genuine or false leads.

5. All about Matthew

Objective

To draw inferences, such as inferring characters' feelings, thoughts and motives from their actions, and justifying them with evidence.

What you need

Copies of *The Goldfish Boy*, photocopiable page 29 'All about Matthew'.

Cross-curricular link

PSHE

What to do

- Tell the children to focus on the character of Matthew. Ask: *What are the two main challenges that Matthew faces?* (overcoming his fear of germs and finding Teddy Dawson)

- Challenge them to explore the emotions that led to his fear of germs (he felt guilty because he believed he had caused Callum's death, and worried he might harm or kill others). Ask: *What emotions drive him in his search for Teddy's kidnapper?* (concern, care for others, perhaps a feeling of guilt that he did not stop it happening) Invite the children to speculate what these feelings tell us about Matthew. (They make his life difficult for him and others, but they show a caring nature.)

- Tell the children that they are going to further explore Matthew's strengths and weaknesses. Arrange them into pairs and hand out photocopiable page 29 'All about Matthew'. Encourage pairs to discuss the questions before completing the page. Bring the class back together to share their findings. Together, explore the reasons behind Matthew's strengths or weaknesses. For example, why do they think he didn't stand up for Jake against the bullies on the bus?

Differentiation

Support: Give children examples of Matthew's behaviour (like standing up for Melody, although failing to stand up for Jake).

Extension: Encourage children to repeat the exercise for other characters.

6. Matthew's places

Objective

To consider how authors have developed settings in what pupils have read.

What you need

Copies of *The Goldfish Boy*, photocopiable page 30 'Matthew's places'.

Cross-curricular link

PSHE

What to do

- With the children, explore the ways the author uses the novel's setting to reflect Matthew's mental health issues. Contrast the novel with an adventure novel which typically travels to wide and varied places. The setting of *The Goldfish Boy* is confined to Matthew's immediate surroundings, in particular, his bedroom and the houses of Chestnut Close. Explain that, in this respect, it is reminiscent of some famous novels and films which are set in a single location, in particular the 1954 film *Rear Window*, a thriller in which the main character witnesses a crime from the window of his apartment (where he is confined with a broken leg). Invite the children to speculate how the confined setting reflects Matthew's problem. (He is trapped by his fear of germs.)

- Arrange the children into pairs and hand out photocopiable page 30 'Matthew's places'. Explain that they should explore how Matthew feels in each setting, referring to the novel and re-reading relevant passages to help them.

- Bring the class back together to share their ideas. Encourage the children to discuss how Matthew's feelings about any of the locations change by the end of the novel. Ask them to provide evidence to back up their ideas.

Differentiation

Support: Discuss one setting as a shared activity before children begin the task.

Extension: Let pairs consider other familiar books which have confined locations (*Kensuke's Kingdom, Holes*).

7. Outsiders

Objectives
To participate in role play; to consider how authors have developed characters in what pupils have read.

What you need
Copies of *The Goldfish Boy*.

Cross-curricular link
PSHE

What to do

- Talk about the three main children featured in the novel: Matthew, Melody and Jake. Discuss what they have in common and what brings them together at the end of the story. (They all feel outsiders because of problems they are grappling with; they come together when they begin to understand each other.)

- Write each character's name on the board. Brainstorm a few words and phrases their peers might use to describe them. (Matthew and Melody could be described as weird, while Jake might be considered a bully.) Discuss briefly key problems each character faces (Matthew's OCD, Melody's parents' break up and Jake's eczema).

- Choose one child to play Matthew. Arrange the other children into two lines, creating a thought tunnel. As 'Matthew' walks through the tunnel, the children on each side should take turns to speak. One side should bully and make fun of Matthew, the other side should show understanding and stand up for him. Before they begin, allow the children time to refer to the novel and think of things they might say. Enact the thought tunnel then invite 'Matthew' to describe how the comments made him feel. Invite the children to repeat the exercise for the character of Jake or Melody.

Differentiation
Support: Prepare for the thought tunnel by making detailed notes on the board about each character and reactions to them.

Extension: Let children repeat the exercise for the third character.

8. Scary settings

Objectives
To consider how authors have developed settings in what pupils have read; to identify and discuss themes and conventions in and across a wide range of writing.

What you need
Copies of *The Goldfish Boy*, photocopiable page 31 'Scary settings'.

What to do

- Write the headings 'Nina's house', 'The graveyard' and 'Dr Kerr's office' on the board and tell the children that they are going to focus on three of the settings outside Chestnut Close which feature in the novel. Invite the children to describe each setting from memory. Brainstorm some adjectives to describe them (spooky, creepy, scary). Ask: *How does Matthew feel when he is in each place?* Encourage the children to support their answers with reasons, for example, Matthew feels uncomfortable in the graveyard because he imagines all the germs that might lurk there.

- Suggest that these are generic scary settings (found in other novels and movies with a scary theme): a spooky old house, a creepy graveyard, a cold and unwelcoming doctor's office or clinic.

- Hand out photocopiable page 31 'Scary settings' and organise the children into pairs to complete the sheet. Bring the class back together to share their findings.

Differentiation
Support: Re-read the relevant passages from the novel together as a class, picking out key descriptive words and phrases and writing them on the board as prompts.

Extension: Working individually, challenge children to choose one of the settings and write a paragraph of description, making it sound as daunting as possible.

All about Matthew

- List examples of Matthew's strengths and weaknesses in each role.

Role	Strengths	Weaknesses
Detective		
Friend		
Son		
Neighbour		

Matthew's places

- Use these words to help you or think of some of your own.

uncomfortable   embarrassed   fidgety   tense   safe   protected   unhappy   worried   panicky

How does Matthew feel when he is…	Briefly explain why he feels this way.
in his bedroom?	
in Dr Rhodes' office?	
at the Mighty Picnic?	
in the graveyard?	

Scary settings

- Authors can use frightening settings such as spooky houses or creepy graveyards to make characters and readers feel nervous or afraid. Explain how each setting features in the novel and how it makes Matthew feel.

Setting	How is it a typical scary theme?	Explain how it features in the novel	Why does Matthew find it scary?
Nina's house			
The graveyard			
Dr Kerr's office			

TALK ABOUT IT ▶

1. The Wallpaper Lion

Objective
To give well-structured descriptions, explanations and narratives for different purposes, including for expressing feelings.

What you need
Copies of *The Goldfish Boy*.

Cross-curricular link
PSHE

What to do

- Tell the children that they are going to focus on the Wallpaper Lion. Ask: *Who or what is he? Why is he important to Matthew?* Arrange the children into pairs and tell them to skim and scan the novel for information about the Wallpaper Lion. Their notes should include what he is and why he is so important to Matthew, how Matthew confides in him and how he helps Matthew. Encourage the children to use bullet points and/or headings to organise their information.

- Give children time to find and note relevant information, then bring the class back together to share their findings. Ask: Why does Matthew need him? (He is solitary, confined to his room; the Wallpaper Lion makes him feel less alone; he is someone to bounce ideas off and so on.) Encourage the children to consider the Wallpaper Lion in the context of an imaginary friend – how sometimes we may need someone to confide in and share our problems with. Remind them how Matthew loses his need for his imaginary friend once he is able to share his problems with his parents and others.

Differentiation
Support: Provide headings to help pairs organise their notes.

Extension: Encourage pairs to explore the concept of imaginary friends in other books and films (*Skellig* by David Almond, *Where The Wild Things Are* by Maurice Sendak).

2. The controller

Objective
To use spoken language to develop understanding through speculating, hypothesising, imagining and exploring ideas.

What you need
Copies of *The Goldfish Boy*, photocopiable page 35 'The controller'.

Cross-curricular link
PSHE

What to do

- Begin by asking the children to suggest coping strategies that Matthew uses to help him manage his anxiety, such as wearing latex gloves, staying in his room and so on. Elicit how all these things help him to feel he is in control. Ask: *Can you recall any times or places in the novel when Matthew does not feel in control and, therefore, becomes anxious?* (when he is in the doctor's waiting room, at the family rounders match or in the graveyard)

- Suggest that when we feel that our lives are out of control, we often react by finding something we have control over. This can result in different kinds of mental health problems such as OCD or an eating disorder. Ask: *Can you think of other behaviours which demonstrate Matthew's desire for control?* (making lists, logging everyday details in his journal) Brainstorm a few ideas and note them on the board.

- Arrange the children into pairs and hand out photocopiable page 35 'The controller'. When they have completed the activity, bring the class back together to share their findings. Reflect how some behaviours, such as excessive hand washing, may be harmful; others, like writing a journal, can be helpful.

Differentiation
Support: Before pairs begin, give them key words to help them identify the behaviours on photocopiable page 35 'The controller'.

Extension: Allow pairs to discuss possible strategies to help Matthew overcome his need for control.

3. Who's guilty?

> **Objective**
> To articulate and justify answers, arguments and opinions.
>
> **What you need**
> Copies of *The Goldfish Boy*.
>
> **Cross-curricular link**
> PSHE

What to do

- Working out who the culprit is, when Teddy Dawson disappears, is one of the leading plot drivers in the novel. Challenge the children to name the characters who become suspects along the way (Melody, Jake, Nina, Mr Jenkins, even Matthew himself). Ask: *Can you name the true culprit?* (Penny) *Can you give two reasons why she took Teddy?* (Penny felt that Mr Charles was not looking after Teddy properly; she hated that her own children had moved away.)

- Arrange the children into small groups. Tell them to discuss whether or not Penny is solely responsible and consider if others might be partly responsible, for example, Mr Charles who was asleep when Teddy was taken.

- Invite children from each group to name characters they feel are partly guilty, giving reasons: Mr Charles neglected his grandson; Melissa Dawson was working rather than taking care of her children; Casey saw Teddy being taken and said nothing; Gordon knew about Penny's guilt and said nothing. Encourage the class to consider whether Matthew feels as if he is partly responsible. Ask: *What do you think?* Encourage them to give reasons for their answers.

> **Differentiation**
>
> **Support:** Provide groups with a list of characters who might bear some responsibility for Teddy's disappearance and challenge them to discuss how.
>
> **Extension:** Encourage groups to discuss whether behaviours can be justified – why might Mr Charles be sleeping? Why might Gordon keep quiet?

4. Fact or opinion?

> **Objectives**
> To distinguish between statements of fact and opinion; to articulate and justify answers, arguments and opinions.
>
> **What you need**
> Copies of *The Goldfish Boy*, photocopiable page 36 'Fact or opinion'.
>
> **Cross-curricular link**
> PSHE

What to do

- Tell the children to focus on the character of Mr Jenkins. Allow them time to refer back to the text and make notes before challenging them to voice short, factual statements about Mr Jenkins. Write their statements on the board, encouraging them to quote from or refer to the text. Ask: *Why does Matthew begin to suspect Mr Jenkins of taking Teddy?* (He knows Mr Jenkins is not as he appears to others; he is a bully behind closed doors and he also secretly smokes, although he likes to present himself as fit and healthy.)

- Arrange the children into pairs and hand out photocopiable page 36 'Fact or opinion?' Give the children time to complete the sheet then bring the class back together to discuss and explain their findings. Ensure that the children have correctly distinguished between statements of fact and opinion. Challenge them to add further statements of fact or opinion, writing them on the board and encouraging them to support their statements with evidence from the novel.

- Allow pairs to repeat the exercise for the character of Old Nina. They should voice statements about her, then, working with their writing partner, they should decide if the statement is fact or opinion.

> **Differentiation**
>
> **Support:** Before they begin, model on the board one fact and one opinion about Mr Jenkins.
>
> **Extension:** Pairs can repeat the exercise for Jake or another character of their choice.

5. A problem shared

Objective
To ask relevant questions to extend their understanding and knowledge.

What you need
Copies of *The Goldfish Boy*.

Cross-curricular link
PSHE

What to do

- Write on the board 'A problem shared is a problem halved.' Ask: *Has anyone heard this saying before? What does it mean?* (Sharing a problem with someone else makes it seem less worrying.) Discuss how the saying applies to Matthew. Ask: *What helps Matthew make a breakthrough in dealing with his fear of germs?* (He confides in Melody and Dr Rhodes and later explains his fears to his parents.)

- Arrange the children into small groups. Ask: *What caused Matthew's fears? Why might he have felt unable to share them before?* They should think about whether Matthew's parents could have done anything differently when they lost the baby or if Matthew could have done anything differently. Encourage the children to explore his reasons for 'bottling it up' or keeping it to himself. (He feels embarrassed, ashamed; he thinks he should deal with it himself.) Bring the class back together and share their ideas. Ask groups to discuss how confiding in others helped Matthew (he learned that he was not guilty for Callum's death) and how others benefit when Matthew confides in them (his parents, Melody and Jake understand his behaviour so they can help him overcome his problems).

Differentiation
Support: Provide groups with a list of prompt questions for discussion.

Extension: Let groups discuss how other characters in the novel might benefit from sharing some of their problems (Old Nina, Jake, Penny).

6. Nina's wisdom

Objectives
To maintain attention and participate actively in collaborative conversations; to discuss and evaluate how authors use language, including figurative language.

What you need
Copies of *The Goldfish Boy*, photocopiable page 37 'Nina's wisdom'.

What to do

- Ask the children if they can recall Nina's advice to Matthew ('Don't ever wait for a storm to pass. You've got to go out there and *dance* in the rain.') Explain that her words are based on a familiar saying. Ask: *Why do you think Nina chooses to say this to Matthew?* (She has faced problems herself and understands that he is struggling.) Ask: *How does Matthew respond?* (He makes himself go to Sue's party.)

- Invite the children to quote other popular weather-related sayings and write them on the board ('Every cloud has a silver lining'; 'It never rains but it pours' and so on). Choose children to explain what they mean and when we might use them. Can they suggest any ways that the sayings could be applied to the novel? For example, 'Every cloud has a silver lining' could be applied to the awful disappearance of Teddy because it brings Matthew, Melody and, later, Jake together as friends.

- Organise the children into pairs and hand out photocopiable page 37 'Nina's wisdom.' Allow them time to complete the sentences, then bring the class back together. Spend time as a class discussing the responses. Encourage and look out for children who respond well to the comments and suggestions of others, for example, by asking relevant questions of the person who has just spoken or by giving reasons for a different response.

Differentiation
Support: Direct children to relevant passages about Nina.

Extension: Challenge pairs to discuss what else Matthew and other characters learn.

The controller

- Explain how Matthew uses the following coping strategies to feel more in control.

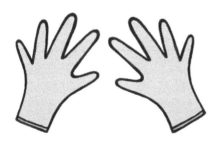

Fact or opinion?

- Decide which statements are fact and which are opinion. Write F or O in the box next to each statement.

Mr Jenkins teaches PE at school. ☐

Mr Jenkins is a secret smoker. ☐

Mr Jenkins is a bully. ☐

Mr Jenkins has very white teeth. ☐

Mr Jenkins is vain. ☐

- Choose two statements of opinion about Mr Jenkins, or write two of your own, and quote evidence from the novel to support them.

1. Mr Jenkins…

_____

_____

_____

_____

2. Mr Jenkins…

_____

_____

_____

_____

Nina's wisdom

- Think about what Old Nina says to Matthew and answer the questions below.

> Don't wait for the storm to pass.
> Go out and dance in the rain.

Explain in one or two sentences what Nina means.

_____

_____

_____

What is 'the rain' in Nina's life?

_____

_____

_____

What does she do to begin 'dancing in the rain'?

_____

_____

_____

Explain 'the rain' in Matthew's life.

_____

_____

_____

How has he been 'waiting for the storm to pass'?

_____

_____

_____

What does Matthew do to begin 'dancing in the rain'?

_____

_____

_____

GET WRITING ▶

1. My room

Objectives
To consider how authors have developed settings in what pupils have read; to describe settings.

What you need
Copies of *The Goldfish Boy*, photocopiable page 41 'My room' – two copies for each child.

What to do
- Write the words 'Prison' and 'Retreat' on the board. Ask: *Where does Matthew spend most of his time?* (in his bedroom) Encourage the children to think about how Matthew's bedroom is represented by both words on the board. (He is confined there by his fears but he also feels relatively safe there.) Ask: *How does he keep it feeling safe?* (constantly cleaning, not allowing people or the cat in)

- Organise the children into pairs and hand out photocopiable page 41 'My room'. Tell the children to skim and scan Chapter 2 for information to help them complete the page. When they have finished, bring the class back together and share their ideas. Ask: *Why is Matthew so familiar with every detail?* (he spends a lot of time there and he is also very observant of detail)

- Using fresh copies of the photocopiable page, challenge the children to work individually to complete the activity again, this time with information about their own bedrooms. Encourage them to include details such as wobbly chair legs or wear on fabric or toys. Then they should use their notes to draft a paragraph describing their bedroom.

Differentiation
Support: Read through Chapter 2 together, extracting key information before pairs begin work.

Extension: Encourage children to extend their paragraph by describing what their room means to them.

2. Clever comparisons

Objectives
To discuss and evaluate how authors use language, including figurative language, considering the impact on the reader; to select appropriate vocabulary, understanding how such choices can change and enhance meaning.

What you need
Copies of *The Goldfish Boy*, photocopiable page 42 'Clever comparisons'.

What to do
- Tell the children that they are going to focus on the author's language, in particular, figurative language. Ask the children if they can recall how Matthew visualises his nagging feeling of guilt (as a black beetle). Read together the passage from Chapter 4, beginning 'The guilt of what I'd done....' as far as '…against an arctic wind.' Ask the children to identify and explain the simile and the metaphor - 'like a vicious black beetle' and 'as though bracing herself against an arctic wind.' Ask: *What do they convey?* Point out how these strong visual images help us to imagine a feeling, a sight or a scene.

- Organise the children into pairs and hand out photocopiable page 42 'Clever comparisons'. When they have completed the page, bring the class back together to share their findings. Broaden the discussion to consider the effect of the descriptive writing in the novel. Ask: *How does it help us to engage with the narrative?* (by visualising the people and places) *How does it reflect Matthew's character?* (These precise visual images are typical of his close observation skills.)

Differentiation
Support: Suggest feelings or places children could create similes for, for example, the lamp in Old Nina's window, an old gravestone.

Extension: Challenge pairs to write more sentences containing metaphors to describe feelings or places featured in the novel.

3. Melody's diary

Objective

To identify the audience for and purpose of the writing, selecting the appropriate form and using other similar writing as models for their own.

What you need

Copies of *The Goldfish Boy.*

What to do

- Together, read Chapter 7 from 'Jake was circling around the road…' to the end of the chapter. Ask a child to summarise the events. (Jake bullies Melody. Matthew rescues her by letting her in but suddenly asks her to leave.) Discuss how Melody feels towards Jake and Matthew, encouraging the children to back up their answers with reasons. (She dislikes Jake because he is a bully; she wants to make friends with Matthew, perhaps because she senses they both need a friend.) Ask: *How does Melody feel as events unfold?* (tense and stressed when Jake blocks her path; pleased and relieved when Matthew 'rescues' her, but upset and confused when he asks her to leave)

- Review key features of diary or journal writing with the children. Remind them that a diary entry uses first-person verbs and is written in the past tense, often in an informal style. Tell the children that they are going to draft a diary entry that Melody might write, summarising what happened with Jake and Matthew. Allow them time to draft their diary entries. Then invite children to read aloud to the class their versions of Melody's diary, encouraging feedback and deciding which are the most convincing and effective.

Differentiation

Support: Draft the first few lines of the diary entry as a class activity then let children develop it.

Extension: Challenge children to write another diary entry for Melody about a different day.

4. Timescales

Objective

To draft and write by précising longer passages.

What you need

Copies of *The Goldfish Boy.*

What to do

- Remind the children how the narrative sometimes shifts back to previous events that happened before the main narrative. Read Chapter 10 together. Challenge the children to identify where the narrative shifts from events that happened previously to the main narrative (Matthew's diary entry). Ask the children what period of time the past events cover, supporting their answers with evidence from the text. Identify and write on the board some time-related phrases from the chapter ('over the weeks', 'That September' and so on).

- As a shared activity, summarise on the board the main events described (Jake's mum and Sue become friends; their babies are born; Jake is found to have allergies and so on). Arrange the children into pairs and challenge them to write a précis of the events in about 100 words. Encourage them to select from the text or add their own time-related words and phrases. Invite children to read their précis aloud, encouraging constructive feedback from the class. Ask: *How much time do you think passes during the main narrative – days, weeks, months?* Encourage the children to cite evidence in support of their answers.

Differentiation

Support: Provide the children with a list of the main events, before they begin their summaries.

Extension: Challenge pairs to draft a summary of events in another chapter, again choosing time-related words and phrases to indicate how much time passes.

5. Front-page news

Objective
To identify the audience for and purpose of the writing, selecting the appropriate form and using other similar writing as models for their own.

What you need
Copies of *The Goldfish Boy*, hard or online copies of local newspaper front pages, photocopiable page 43 'Front-page news'.

Cross-curricular link
PSHE

What to do

- Remind the children of the television reporter who reports on Teddy's disappearance. Tell them that they are going to plan and write a report for the front page of the local newspaper. They will need to think about the facts of the story, a few neighbours they might interview, a headline and the photographs they will use.

- Arrange the children into pairs and hand out photocopiable page 43 'Front-page news'. Remind them to refer to the novel to help them find relevant information. When they have finished, come together as a class to share their ideas for headlines and quotes and to review the key facts for the story. If possible, view headlines about disappearances or missing persons in local newspapers online or in print, being aware of local issues and children's sensitivities.

- Working individually, the children should then write their newspaper reports. Allow time for them to compare their report with a partner and then ask them to spend time editing to improve it. Invite children to read their reports aloud to the class and encourage constructive feedback.

Differentiation
Support: Brainstorm on the board key facts and possible interviewees before pairs begin work.

Extension: Allow children to use their IT skills to develop their stories.

6. Dr Rhodes' report

Objective
To use organisational and presentational devices to structure text and to guide the reader (for example, headings, bullet points, underlining).

What you need
Copies of *The Goldfish Boy*.

Cross-curricular link
PSHE

What to do

- Ask: *What is Dr Rhodes' role in the novel?* (She is a therapist who is trying to help Matthew overcome his OCD.) Explain to the children that they are going to plan and draft a report that Dr Rhodes might write about Matthew at the end of his sessions with her. They should begin by re-reading Chapters 14 and 36 where Matthew's sessions with Dr Rhodes are described. Working in pairs, they should then plan a structure for their report. Remind the children to think about how Dr Rhodes would organise her notes. Brainstorm a few ideas and write them on the board, for example: name, age, problem, symptoms, suggested diagnosis and so on.

- Allow the children time to work on their plans then challenge them to work individually to draft their reports. Encourage them to refer to their plans and add underlining and bullet points for a clear and concise presentation. They should also consider vocabulary choice and grammar, as this is a formal report by a doctor. Invite volunteers to present their reports to the class, encouraging feedback on which are the most effective and why.

Differentiation
Support: Provide a list of headings for pairs to use to help plan their reports.

Extension: Challenge children to write a letter from Dr Rhodes to Matthew's parents explaining her findings and recommendations.

 # My room

- Describe the view you can see from the window.

_____

_____

_____

_____

_____

- Describe the décor and features.

_____

_____

_____

_____

_____

- List and briefly describe any belongings.

_____

_____

_____

_____

_____

- My rules and regulations.

_____

_____

_____

_____

_____

 # Clever comparisons

- Draw a line to match the simile to the feeling or thing it describes.

The roses in Mr Charles' garden	like a blazing sun
Casey's doll	like tight bundles of pink candyfloss
Mr Charles' head	like a vicious black beetle
The Wallpaper Lion's mane	like a doomed heroine
The breeze	like a hot hairdryer
Matthew's guilt	like a tanned walnut

- Think of two things that the beetle simile suggests about Matthew's feeling of guilt:

    1. _____

    _____

    2. _____

    _____

- Write three more sentences containing similes to describe other feelings or places featured in the book.

_____

_____

_____

_____

_____

_____

Front-page news

- Use this page to plan a newspaper report about the disappearance of Teddy Dawson.

Write your headline here: _____

_____

Describe two photographs you will use:

1. A person _____

2. A place _____

List four key facts about Teddy's disappearance:

1. _____

2. _____

3. _____

4. _____

Interviewees

Name	Who are they?	What they said

ASSESSMENT ▶

1. Six questions

> ### Objective
> To ask questions to improve their understanding.
>
> ### What you need
> Copies of *The Goldfish Boy*.

What to do

- Tell the children that they are going to compile multiple-choice quiz questions about the novel to challenge other groups or teams. Organise them into small groups and give them time to compile a quiz of six multiple-choice questions. Children should skim and scan the novel for ideas for their questions. They should appoint one note taker to write down their questions and another to keep a list of correct answers.

- Before they begin, model an example on the board and challenge the children to provide the answer. For example,

  For Halloween Matthew dressed as:
  a.   An alien
  b.   A werewolf
  c.   A vampire   Answer: b.

- When they have finished, they should challenge other groups to take part in their quiz. Review the scores and announce the winning groups. Encourage feedback from the class, identifying which quiz questions are the most challenging and why.

> ### Differentiation
> **Support:** Let children base their quiz questions on one topic such as Teddy's disappearance.
>
> **Extension:** Let groups devise an alternative quiz such as a true or false quiz about the novel to challenge other groups.

2. Possibilities

> ### Objective
> To use modal verbs or adverbs to indicate degrees of possibility.
>
> ### What you need
> Copies of *The Goldfish Boy*.

What to do

- Revise modal verbs with the children. Begin by writing a list on the board (can/could, may/might, will/would, shall/should/must). Then ask: *Can you name all the characters in the novel whom Matthew suspects are involved in Teddy's disappearance?* List them on the board: Mr Charles, Casey, Mr Jenkins, Old Nina, Melody, Jake, Penny.

- Working in pairs, invite the children to work through the list of suspects, writing a short sentence about each one and using a modal verb each time. Each sentence should begin: Matthew thinks [name of suspect] [modal verb] be guilty because…. Model an example on the board: 'Matthew thinks Casey may be guilty because she pushed him in the pond.'

- Encourage the children to experiment with different modal verbs, deciding which work best in their sentences. When they have finished, bring the class back together and invite children to read their sentences aloud. Compare sentences about the same character, encouraging feedback.

- Review how the modal verbs can suggest how likely Matthew thinks something is, for example, Matthew thinks Mr Charles *could* be guilty because he is tired of looking after the children; Matthew thinks Penny *must* be guilty because he sees the toddler's sticky handprint on her door.

> ### Differentiation
> **Support:** Perform the task as a shared spoken activity.
>
> **Extension:** Challenge children to change their sentences into the past tense (Matthew thought…) using the correct modals.

3. What's it all about?

> **Objective**
> To identify and discuss themes and conventions in and across a wide range of writing.
>
> **What you need**
> Copies of *The Goldfish Boy*.
>
> **Cross-curricular link**
> PSHE

What to do

- Ask: *What are the main themes in the novel?* (struggling with a mental health problem, feeling an outsider, solving a crime) Write on the board the children's ideas, prompting them with questions as necessary. (What challenges does Matthew face? What dramatic events happen in the neighbourhood?)

- If the children have recently read any other novels that cover similar themes (for example, children facing mental health issues, or a young detective solving a crime) invite comparisons, focusing on key features such as narrator, plot and style. Encourage subjective opinion (I think this novel is interesting because… This novel is unusual because…).

- Ask the children to choose the theme they think is most significant or has the most impact on them. They should write a short statement beginning: I think *The Goldfish Boy* is a novel about… They should describe the theme and why they think it is important. For example, I think *The Goldfish Boy* is a novel about feeling an outsider because Matthew, Melody and Jake all feel as if they are outsiders. Invite volunteers to read aloud their statements and encourage feedback from the class.

> **Differentiation**
> **Support:** Provide a list of main themes and ask children to choose the one they think is most significant and write a statement explaining why.
>
> **Extension:** Challenge children to construct mind maps, plotting the main themes in the novel and including notes about each theme.

4. What's so important?

> **Objective**
> To articulate and justify answers, arguments and opinions.
>
> **What you need**
> Copies of *The Goldfish Boy*, flash cards with the names of Matthew, Melody, Dr Rhodes, Penny and Teddy on them, a stopwatch, photocopiable page 47 'What's so important?'.

What to do

- Tell the children that they are going to summarise as concisely as possible how each key character is important to the plot. Explain that as you hold up a flash card with a character's name on it, children should explain in under 30 seconds how they are important to the plot. They should follow the sentence pattern: 'X is important to the plot because…' Model an example for them: 'Teddy is important to the plot because someone kidnaps him and Matthew has to try to find out who took him.' For each character, invite a child to begin the challenge. Then encourage others to add ideas, again working against the stopwatch.

- Tell the children that they are now going to repeat the exercise, focusing on objects that feature in the plot. Hand out photocopiable page 47 'What's so important?' and give them time to complete it. Bring the class back together and invite volunteers to read their explanations. Challenge them to consider how each object relates to or helps develop the key themes in the novel.

> **Differentiation**
> **Support:** Working as a class, allow children to attempt the 30-second challenge as a spoken exercise for the objects on the photocopiable page before they begin writing.
>
> **Extension:** Challenge children to extend their work on the photocopiable sheet by adding further objects and explaining their significance.

5. Matthew's journey

Objective
To draft and write by précising longer passages.

What you need
Copies of *The Goldfish Boy*.

Cross-curricular link
PSHE

What to do

- Explain to the children that they are going to consider and summarise all the different things that Matthew learns during the course of the novel. Write on the board 'The novel is set in Chestnut Close, but Matthew goes on a journey.' Ask: *How does Matthew go on a journey without leaving his neighbourhood?* Suggest that the idea of a journey can be used as a metaphor for what Matthew experiences and learns.

- Working in pairs, challenge the children to identify the goal or destination of Matthew's journey. (He wants to achieve a more normal life, overcome his OCD and also solve the mystery of Teddy's disappearance.) They should list all the things Matthew learns on his journey. As a class, brainstorm some topics to consider and write them on the board: things about himself, his strengths and weaknesses, friendships, how to get through difficult times and so on. Encourage them to use headings, underlining and bullet points to organise their key ideas.

- Bring the class back together and invite pairs of children to share their findings, consolidating key points in a bulleted list on the board.

Differentiation

Support: Provide a list of prompt questions for children to answer: what does Matthew learn about himself/friendships/how to get through difficult times?

Extension: Let children work individually to write a paragraph explaining how Matthew goes on a journey while staying at home.

6. Chapter clues

Objective
To use organisational and presentational devices to structure text and to guide the reader (for example, headings, bullet points, underlining).

What you need
Copies of *The Goldfish Boy*.

What to do

- Tell the children that they are going to use the author's chapter titles to review the way the novel is structured. Ask the children to pick out some examples to explain the content behind the title, for example, Chapter 10 'Jake's story' tells us that we are going to learn more about the character of Jake and what has happened to him in the past. Chapter 28 'The police visit old Nina' tells us that the police are going to follow up on Matthew's suspicions and investigate Nina to see if she is guilty of taking Teddy.

- Challenge the children to work in pairs to select and organise chapter titles into categories, for example, titles focusing on characters ('Jake', 'Penny Sullivan'), titles focusing on places ('The rectory'; 'The graveyard') or titles focusing on events ('The sleepover'; 'The arrest'). Tell them to use headings, underlining and bullet points to help organise their lists.

- Bring the class back together to review their work. Consider together how much the titles tell us about the content of the chapter and what they contribute to the novel, highlighting key characters, places and events.

Differentiation

Support: Provide categories for children to organise titles into.

Extension: Challenge children to write the synopsis for an additional chapter, giving it a title in keeping with the novel.

What's so important?

- Briefly explain how each of these objects features in the plot.

Choose one item which you think is most important in driving the plot and explain why.

_____

_____

_____

SCHOLASTIC
READ & RESPOND

Available in this series:

978-1407-18325-1

978-1407-17510-2

978-1407-17616-1

978-1407-17615-4

978-1407-18324-4

978-1407-17506-5

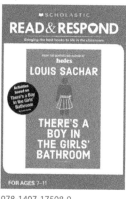

978-1407-17508-9

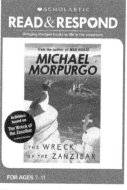

978-1407-17509-6

978-1407-17617-8

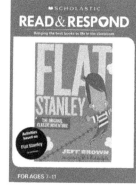

978-1407-17618-5

978-1407-18248-3

978-1407-18247-6

978-1407-18250-6

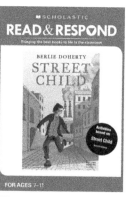

978-1407-18251-3

978-1407-18252-0

978-1407-18253-7

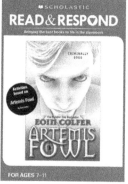

978-1407-18255-1

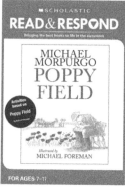

978-1407-18323-7

978-1407-18383-1

978-1407-18394-7

To find out more, call 0845 6039091
or visit our website www.scholastic.co.uk/readandrespond